Kissimmee Pete
and the
Hurricane

Kissimmee Pete
and the
Hurricane

By Jan Day

Illustrated by Janeen Mason

PELICAN PUBLISHING COMPANY

GRETNA 2008

To Alicia and Alan, with love.
—Jan Day

To Floridians and our colorful past, and to Jan Day
for keeping our imaginations alive.
With love,
— JM

The word "Pelican" and the depiction of a pelican
are trademarks of Pelican Publishing Company, Inc.,
and are registered in the U.S. Patent and Trademark Office.

Library of Congress Cataloging-in-Publication Data

Day, Jan, 1943-
  Kissimmee Pete and the hurricane / by Jan Day ; illustrated by Janeen Mason.
    p. cm.
  Summary: In the late 1800s, Kissimmee Pete, cracker cow hunter, stands up to a hurricane that threatens his herd of cattle and the people, buildings, animals, and plants of Punta Rassa, Florida. Includes facts about Florida history and hurricanes.
  ISBN 978-1-58980-544-6 (hardcover : alk. paper) [1. Cowboys—Fiction. 2. Hurricanes—Fiction. 3. Florida—History—19th century—Fiction. 4. Tall tales.] I. Mason, Janeen I., ill. II. Title.
  PZ7.D3315Kip 2008
  [E]--dc22

                              2008008667

Printed in Korea
Published by Pelican Publishing Company, Inc.
1000 Burmaster Street, Gretna, Louisiana 70053

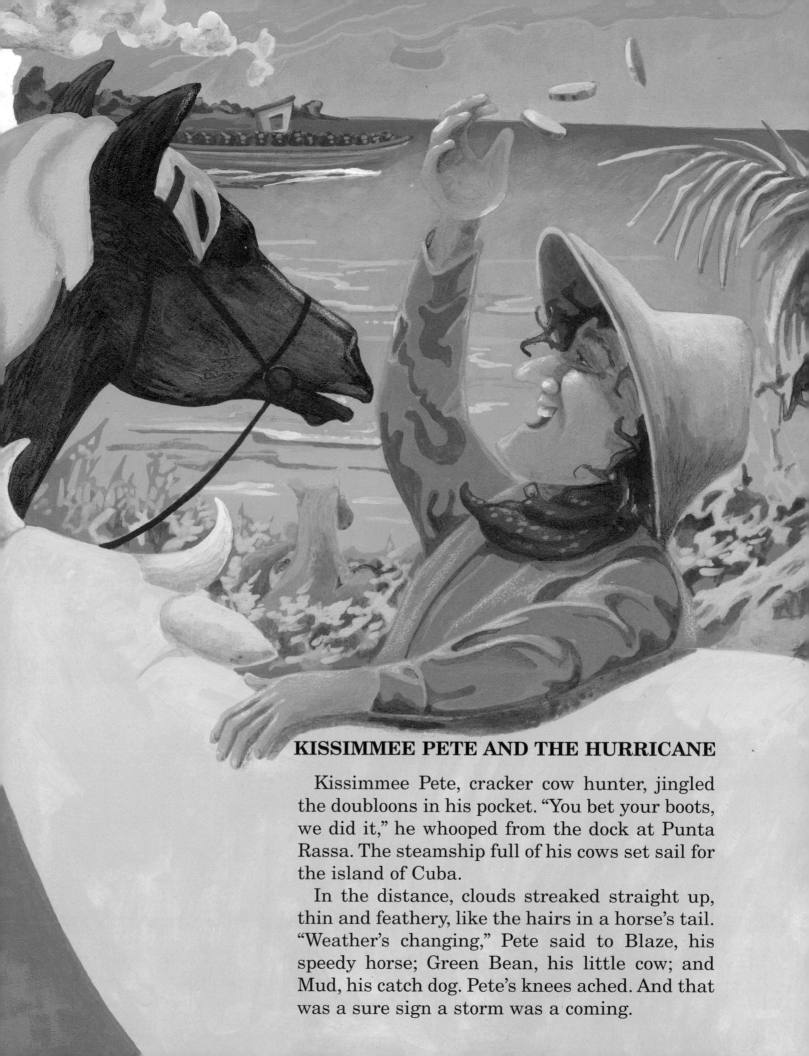

KISSIMMEE PETE AND THE HURRICANE

Kissimmee Pete, cracker cow hunter, jingled the doubloons in his pocket. "You bet your boots, we did it," he whooped from the dock at Punta Rassa. The steamship full of his cows set sail for the island of Cuba.

In the distance, clouds streaked straight up, thin and feathery, like the hairs in a horse's tail. "Weather's changing," Pete said to Blaze, his speedy horse; Green Bean, his little cow; and Mud, his catch dog. Pete's knees ached. And that was a sure sign a storm was a coming.

A Seminole man rolled by with his family in a wagon. He pointed east. "Saw grass is bloomin'. Evil spirits will blow in here before you know it."

Pete didn't believe in evil spirits, but when he saw a flock of ibis trailing behind the Seminoles, he thought he'd better get moving. Ibis were the last to flee before a hurricane hit. "We got to get out of here," Pete shouted.

Dark clouds raced in. Waves rose to lick the sky. One gigantic blast flung the steamship right back to shore. Pete's cows huddled in the bow. The gusts were so strong it drove one cow's spots off her back and smack onto Green Bean.

"Looks like somebody whacked you with a bucket of paint," Pete howled above the roar of the wind. "Now you look more like the other cows."

"Watch out for them waves," Pete hollered, just as monster swells swept the cows clean off the steamship and straight down Main Street into the fancy new Kingfish Inn. Mud tried to head them off, but before Pete could yell, "Get 'em," Mud and those cows were hanging out the windows.

A burst of wind caught the hotel roof, and it soared out to sea. Walls collapsed, and cows went sailing down the road in chairs, on tables, and in beds. Mud clung to a pillow. A tenderfoot tourist rode a wild door. A tarpon swam up the street. Later Pete would say the hurricane blew so hard that it shoved August straight into December without even stopping for Halloween or Thanksgiving.

Pete and Mud rounded up the cows and headed inland, but the more the hurricane roared, the angrier he got. "Hold on a minute, you ornery old spot remover." Pete yelled, shaking his fist at the sky. But the wind had a mind of its own and socked him off Blaze.

Madder than ever, Pete grabbed his cow whip and slashed at the biggest thundercloud. "I'm going to chop you up so you can't do any more damage." Pete snarled at the hurricane.

But the louder he snapped his whip, the more the lightning boomed back. Once Pete thought he'd been shot at by a cannon.

The sky grew blacker than a big bear's back. The racket liked to deafen the squirrels hiding out under moon vine in the custard apple trees. The hurricane swirled, slammed, and shook everything in four counties.

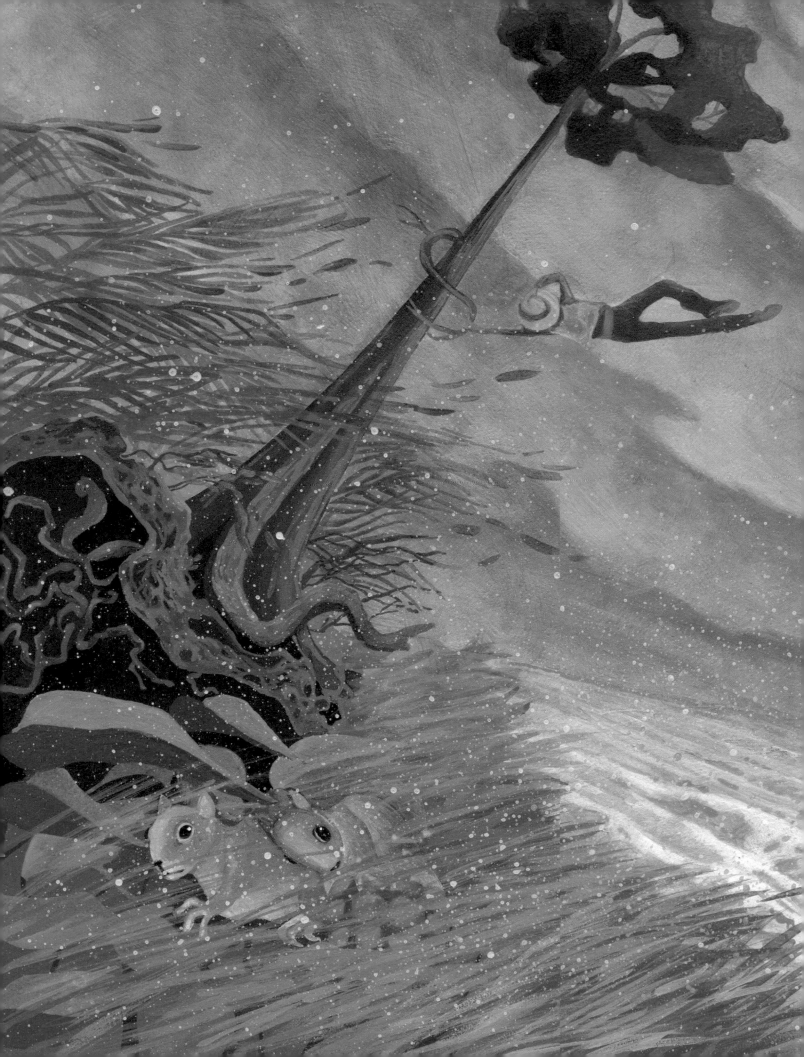

Faster than you can say "Yeehaw," Green Bean, Mud, and Blaze, and the cows were blown over Lake Okeechobee. But Pete grabbed on to a tree. The tree slowed him down, but the wind did not intend to leave Pete unmoved. It blew Pete and the tree as far as the western shore. Lake Okeechobee was so shallow that the waves laid closer together than bacon in a fry pan. It would be mighty tough swimming across miles of choppy water.

Pete pushed against wind as riled up as cows in the middle of a stampede. When he got down to the cattails at the edge of the lake, he found two of the biggest alligators he'd ever seen. "Hi, fellers, time to do some sightseeing!" Pete tied one alligator to each foot and took off rip-roaring across the lake. "Giddyup," he bellowed. The alligators' noses were just right for navigating white caps. Their tails slapped faster than any oar.

Finally, the gators dumped Pete near the mouth of the Kissimmee River. He found Blaze, Green Bean, Mud, and the cows hiding in a saw palmetto patch. The alligators raced off without a thought of steak for lunch.

All of a sudden the strong winds stopped. The blue eye of the hurricane gleamed overhead.

Pete herded the cows along the Kissimmee River, hoping to reach high ground before the storm started blowing again. Green Bean remembered her first bath in the river and hopped right in for a dip.

"Get out of there," Pete ordered. "This is no time for sprucin' up."

The river spilled over its banks and onto the
flood plain even though the sun was still shining.
A capsized ferry drifted across. Only a panther
and her kittens got a ride. Two gray foxes
stretched out on a logjam that drifted from the
sawmill just up the way.

People ran out of their homes to rescue cows and horses. Some of the houses had lost roofs and doors. Pots and pans and boots and buckets bobbed in the water. Mud nabbed a puppy inside a bonnet and drug it to shore.

Old Mrs. Quick paddled her boat as fast as she could, determined to save the quilt she'd been working on for her granddaughter's wedding gift. Abigail Johnson yanked on her pet pig stuck on a sandbar. Ibis soared out of a lean red maple, then turned and flew into the sturdy cypress.

Pete looked at the clear sky and shook his head. Folks had forgotten that once the eye passed, the hurricane would wallop them again from the opposite direction. Even at that moment, the water was rising.

"Get that tub of lard moving," Pete thundered at Abigail. Some folks say Pete roared so loud that he woke up the hurricane. He sure scared the pig.

"Go on home. That storm ain't done with us yet," he screamed at everyone, but they were too worried about their animals to pay him any mind.

Pete put his brain to use again. He rounded up Blaze, Green Bean, Mud, and the cows. They dove into the river and pushed the logjam toward the shore. "Help us build a dam," Pete called to a family of passing otters. The otters dug out a place for the logs and shoved them in. "That'll hold the water back for a spell," Pete said. Oxbows formed where the river had run off course.

But not everyone made it to higher ground before the river began to spill over the dam. Pete had to do something and fast. He blew out all his breath and then sucked in the rising water. In one gigantic spout, he spit it into a valley ten miles away. Pretty little Lake Istokpoga is still there to this day.

Just when everyone began to feel safe, the hurricane sped back across the flood plain, and sure enough, it was from the opposite direction.

"You old wind bag. You won't get us this time." Pete grabbed his cow whip again, cracking it louder and higher than ever. With a flick of his wrist, he hurled that hurricane right out to sea.

Tomorrow Pete would drive the cows back to port.

That night the whole valley celebrated. Abigail came with her pet pig dressed in its best Sunday hat. Mrs. Quick served up sweet potato pie and swamp cabbage stew. Mud, Blaze, and Green Bean sang a moonlight serenade. Everyone cheered and hooted and declared Kissimmee Pete the greatest cracker hero ever.

Did You Know?

Spanish explorer Juan Ponce de León brought cows, horses, and citrus to Florida in 1521.

When the pilgrims landed at Plymouth Rock, the Spanish cowboys were already in Florida.

Cow hunters used long whips to run the cows out of the brush. The cracking sound of their whips earned them the name of "cracker cow hunters".

In the late 1800s, ranchers and cattle brought people to central Florida. They faced rustlers just like ranchers in the frontier west.

An oxbow is a U-shaped bend in a river. When the Kissimmee River flooded, new channels formed cutting off these oxbows and creating oxbow lakes.

A flood plain is a low plain or valley floor formed by a river and floods and is under water part of the year.

Wetlands are also under water part of the year and create a habitat, or home, for many fish and other wildlife. Marshes and swamps are the two main types of wetlands.

In the late 1800s, when Pete's story takes place, the Kissimmee River meandered about 103 miles from Lake Kissimmee to Lake Okeechobee through a one- to two-mile-wide flood plain. The flood plain was covered with 35,000 acres of wetlands.

Lake Okeechobee is the second largest freshwater lake located entirely within the United States. Lake Michigan is the first.